AF477912

I'M AMAZED THAT YOU'RE STILL SINGING

Jack Myers

I'm Amazed That You're Still Singing

L'Epervier Press

Acknowledgements

Some of these poems first appeared in *The American Poetry Review, Cedar Rock, The Chariton Review, Cimarron Review, Columbia, The Georgia Review, The Iowa Review, The Missouri Review, The North American Review, The Ohio Review, Quarterly West, Seneca Review, Southern Poetry Review, Three Sisters, The Texas Review, The Virginia Quarterly Review*, and *Vision* magazine.

"Day of Atonement" first appeared in the anthology VOICES WITHIN THE ARK: MODERN JEWISH POETS.

"Sleep" first appeared in the anthology TEXAS STORIES AND POEMS.

"Before Making Love to Me" and "Too Many Miles of Sunlight Between Us" first appeared in THE ANTHOLOGY OF MAGAZINE VERSE AND YEARBOOK OF POETRY, 1980.

"Winging It" first appeared in the anthology THE POET'S CHOICE.

The poet sincerely thanks Southern Methodist University and the Corporation of Yaddo for granting him time and space in which to write some of these poems.

Copyright 1981 by Jack Myers

Library of Congress Cataloging in Publication Data
Myers, Jack Elliott, 1941-
    I'm amazed that you're still singing.

    I. Title.
PS3563.Y42I4   811'.54   81-8452
ISBN 0-934332-35-5   AACR2
ISBN 0-934332-34-7 (pbk.)

Cover photograph by David Akiba
Back cover photograph by Peter Feldman
Book design by Bridget Culligan
Typography by Maggie Checkoway Howell

The publication of this book was made possible in part with a grant from the National Endowment for the Arts, a federal agency.

L'Epervier Press books are available at your local bookstore or may be ordered from Small Press Distribution, 1784 Shattuck Avenue, Berkeley, California 94709.

L'EPERVIER PRESS

Dedicated to the memory of my mother

Ruth Myers

CONTENTS

4.   Call to be Left in the Air

5.   Living Alone

1. The Immigrants

These are home-lost people.
Their house has left them—
Not all at once, but each stone at its time,
Each tile, each curtain, each word.

And the shape of forgetting
Is like lips closed, humming.

— Yehuda Amichai

Day of Rest

When mother lit the candles on a Friday night
the bull plunging through the rooms all week lay down.
Even the gulls settled down like papers on the breakers.
The Sabbath was the torch she swept her house with.

In those days it was simple: a sip of wine rushed us
through ourselves and we were blessed. The stars
came out like little sayings: Be good. Be good.
It was nothing to touch a God.

But it isn't like that now. The afternoons rise up
like the cement sides of an empty sea and filling up
on booze, I become the bull. Knock the daylight down.
The walls redden with laughter as I wake with someone
holding down my fists.

Some Friday night, my last, will find me glazed and stiff.
The light pinched out, last thoughts smoking up
as if I were a wick. Somewhere a woman will be lighting
candles and children drinking wine. God bless.
All night there will be a melting into space,
a long, slow leap toward God.

Day of Atonement

On the Day of Atonement we fasted
and threw our money into the sea;
a few faces bright with guilt
went up against the wind
and fell like sinful children
without a splash.

Eventually we lugged God down there
and dumped him in.
It changed the taste of the sea.

Those cold October afternoons seemed carved
out of the light and wind howling
through the ram's horn. Each dry blast
was a mountain in Israel. A word.

When the emptiness in us folded
its corners into a heavy silver star,
we doubled over and feasted on resentment.
Everything taught us how to win.

Once we whispered to each cent
a sin. Now money whispers back.
The emptiness that drilled us out
has hungered, blackened, knotted into sex
until we think of hauling our belongings
down to the sea and following them in.

The waves scrub the sea from Israel
to our feet, as we sway above our lives,
ablaze, wondering how to throw the light in.

Payment

You learn to walk over your own heart in this life.
You learn to shout get out. Everything you buy
you put black dogs around and let them pound the air.

You know what an old man washes up in? Laughter.
That's what he collects. Give me the money!
In it goes, then I get some rest. Let the waves lower
their heads and ram the walls. Tomorrow I'll collect.

On some days I just sit. I make everything empty.
My children are away, grown. I can't pull down their masks.
Even the children looking in this house, who could be killers,
think they are sneaking up on death. So I turn on them,
the little seagulls, like this—!
Ah well, it gives me a little pleasure.

But never in my life did I raise my fist.
Except to make a deal. My father smashed this table
and his meal, plate and all, stuck to the ceiling
like a fixture. No one said a word. To this day,
when I shake hands with a man, as God is my witness,
I look up and see it there.

So now I'm old. What else? My pains could fill a house.
I feel them sending messages like stars in the flesh
as I schlep around under memories and complain.
I ask you, who could allow mirrors in such a house?

You, tell me please, what should I turn into?
Someone nice? Put new wood in the rain
and it turns black. It's junk. When I drop dead
the house will fall on top of me. Burn it up.
Let the dogs howl for their meal. No one will collect.

What's Left

Today I'm going into town to give away what's left.
I drag my memory down like a black wool suit,
let the dead air disrobe from the last sad occasion,
yawn, and inhale the house. It held me as my woman
held me, while the shadows fell and filled my shape.

In the market they will ask did I ever face my life.
Yes, I say. I sat inside it. Only backwards. I watched
the beginning being crushed by landscapes rushing toward it.
Now I toss that in for free, a black dot impossible to lift.

I see the few small things I've gathered in the wagon
make a quiet music. Moored on the warm river in the wood
they nod in the mild wind like grown men settling down,
then they change back into things I can't tell from myself.

At my age I should have one last child and face him
like a mountain. Blind and deaf. Tell him it's easy
to learn when there's nothing left. All this I hitch up
to a strong dumb horse. He will pull it twitching into town,
bearing high his faceful of flies like a torch.

Still Life

An old woman sits facing the continual explosion of the sun,
flicking her arthritic wrists back and forth like fiery bracelets,
letting the sun burn a scorchmark of her image on the wall
like those shadows at Hiroshima, locked between oblivion and
      surprise.
Wiping her nose, she endures dead ones fallen all the way back
to Russia, snow swirling through the empty streets of Minsk.

It's not a question of love anymore. She's seen love rot.
Sunk against herself, she lets the sun sink into her and rise
over and over again like wine. She sits there on fire riding out
the last inch of her history, nodding to the paperboy who cycles by
hurling news of the world at the world: It will not give up.

Scissors Sharpener

Before the light
behind the sea displays its row of open scissors,
I'm pulling on my pants. It's a miracle how they complete me.
Each crease is a long story and I remember who I am.
I dream I'm soaking in a tub over a glass of steaming tea
before I push the streets wide open
chanting scissors, scissors.

Look at the fools
splashing in the icy sea. They think they can jump back
into themselves, wake up from this life. As if they could
lose themselves, they keep on swimming until they're afraid
of getting lost. But to me, one splash from my basin
and I'm direct from the Black Sea.

I'm used to myself here,
snoring like a grindstone, arms strong as wagon handles,
my mouth wide open as a bell. Women look out the window
asking what's all the commotion and see me cutting through
a rag in mid-air. In my business, whatever I sharpen,
no one needs me for a year.

I should start.
When you finally learn everything there is to know,
you're ready to drop dead. You get so you don't hear
the wheel, the bell, the talk. You begin to believe,
the minute you walk away, everything in the world
is going dull.

The Butcher's Hand

After she executed the laundry
high over an alley, left steam
clinging to the wall,
and transmogrified the hamburg,
my mother called the butcher,
"Cheat, you goddamn thief,"
while I faded through my haze
of prickles as the go-between.

Imagine telling a blood-smeared man
"You're eating out my heart!"
A pound of fresh ground beef
rolled in agony around my basket
as I rode the blood-soaked bag
back. "My mother says this time
you better take your hand off
the scale." I slide along the saw-
dust covered floor, past tongues,
livers, and headless chickens.

Years later I saw my mother's rage
was the rage of the weak, the defeated;
that the butcher heard only drab birds
squawking in the kingdom of disbelief.
Her smashing in the kitchen,
the water rushing into the house,
and the long sigh of exhaustion
when I opened the door was my family
falling like a pound of meat
into the butcher's hand.

Louie the Fruitman

You're a seed clinging to the inside
of your store, moaning, "Oy, what impossible prices."

You might as well be crying you're unborn:
that's the recognition your eyes tear from me.

And the dark eye of your heavy wife, spying through
a bagel, listening to your name slide out

from someone's mouth like heart failure.
It makes her nauseous.

Life could have been for you a wagon loaded down
with bright fruit. But it was highway robbery,

God stabbing you in the chest with a customer's
finger, the kids under an avalanche of apples.

You got so cheap you tried to shave a nickel
from my change. Don't break my heart for a nickel,

you'd say, checking to see if the cash register
still shone six feet off the floor.

I'm grown now, Louie. I can hold the carved head
of a pumpkin in one hand. I'm thinking about you

smashing open an orange with revenge, squeezing out
the pulp when a customer refused to pay the extra dime.

I'm beating you out the front door into traffic,
tearing off your favorite Hawaiian shirt.

Now we can both call for the cops.
We can both claim we've been robbed.

Hand-Me-Down

Plenty of days he was curled over a bowl of thin soup
with the electric bill glaring up from the table,
when his muscles were so dry he felt crisscrossed by leashes.
But tonight he's dancing with his wife and the whole extended family
claps in time. There is something about tomorrow in his dare,
something of an incoming bird.

I stand in the silo of myself watching the skinny flicker
of his legs go off like firecrackers among the children.
He feels netted in a dim starlight of his pains.
They remind him of constellations. It helps him to sleep.

Weightless as a mild thought, his forehead has settled
over mine. I always thought it was a hill some last survivor
would have to climb. And so I stumble in his heavy winter coat;
strange bondage to find myself in my grandfather's shy body,
looking up, wishing again for what? I don't even have words for myself.

The Immigrant

Before I knew your word for *Fall,*
the trees let go beyond the window.
I thought I was rising as the season explained
itself, leaving the streets littered with words.

Then on an August afternoon miles out
on a motionless sea, I lowered down a dropline.
A large cod tugged my hand into the water,
forcing me to see the ripples thin out of sight
until I was staring across the ocean to the east,
feeling it sift through what light was left around me.

That was *evening.* It was like looking into
a woman's eyes and being pulled inside her.
And I could break it by swallowing
just as the free cod had broken the water
far from my boat. It is impossible to describe
the bareness and dark I drifted through that *night,*
totally outside myself, except to say everything
calms down and becomes whole whenever it offers itself.

There are many other words in the last half of my life
I will learn.

2. To A Distant Lover

The wild animal trainer says
he aims to teach his lions
and tigers only fear and respect.
Love, he says, is too dangerous.

— Ernest Sandeen

Let's do the dance we do.
Let's irrigate this place.
When you hold your arms above your head
and throw a proud hip out, that singer
get the music blown back in his face.
Let's do the dance we do.

Others shaking their heads at the struggles
we go through, though we dance in place,
don't see this reeling as a reaching
toward ourselves. What I feel is so different
from what the mirror says, I have to touch
my face. Who cares what's real? Let's do
the dance we do.

When we do this dance have I forgotten
or remembered who I am? The ever-changing
spaces that we fast-dance through, exactly
do the dance we do. Let's hold this music
without ever letting go. But if it goes
just snap your fingers one by one and tell me
that by letting go, we'll keep the music
and the dance we do. Let's do the dance
we do.

Before Making Love to Me,

she dances the Tai Chi naked,
turning our room 3,000 years old.

The long wind coming toward us
has arrived and I have the feeling

cats are in the room, though nothing
but the moon's white hexagram

has entered through the blinds.
She is sideways in Egyptian relief,

perhaps letting go of birds.
Her breasts dip upward as if just

touched. Her mind is all at once
stills of pouring water, a halted rain

of arrows in a lion, the roar of silence
steaming from an offered dish. I am no more

myself than my clothes hanging in the dark
blue air. She is against me now, as we

move toward making love. The silence,
over the slow explosion of ourselves,

rises and falls like blows.

Bringing Up the Sun

When Hope opened her bathrobe
the light went through me like a heart attack.
The room leaned inward and I lunged
against myself, rolling over everything
to pull her down.

She was just another woman
who could turn the earth over
with my buried face.

On the smooth warm rocks
she'd look into me and say: No one's home.
Then we'd push through whole
summer afternoons in bed, high
over the gaiety of the beach crowds.

Then one Sunday a white Cadillac
loaded with Greeks and loud music
pulled up. Hope looked into the sun
like the sun, then jumped in.

She married and stuffed herself
into a small apartment where
disappointment falls from the shelves
like food she thought she didn't have.

And I carry her name among the cries
of the exiles bringing up the sun.

To a Distant Lover

It is said
the Zen Archer
never takes a shot
but allows the center
of his target
to expand
until it is night
and small holes
like stars
his arrows
might go through
burst into suns
stuck with arrows.

In the white light
of this night
the Zen Master
becomes
a bow,
an arrow,
the very center
of the target
he flies through.

Accomplishing everything
within nothing,
he complains,
is an exercise
he still must do.

A hundred miles away,
day and night
with one eye closed,
I concentrate on you.

Thanksgiving Day

The light hooves that I flashed on have softened into shoes
now that you've gone. Today was a plunge down a black shaft:
headaches, things shrinking into absences, ticks. I am waiting
for the long sonic boom of your wake to pass.

My parents called today and asked me how I am. Boxcars and boxcars
of blunt questions have been clacking over me, so I've lost
even the feel of what I am. In a few days, you'll drive back
and knock me out again.

My other woman waits, watching me wobble through this
mucoid silence, watching me stutter out of coincidence
with myself. If I slept with her now, I'd rage through her
mild body or hold on clonicly for days. Though we never speak
of sex, her face, when she tries facing me, says no.
Any word I chose would bare the studding in the walls.

When you come back, you'll wear the same loose fitting dress
that punished me, that made me pinwheel inside—Why
isn't everyone falling? These words will have been sifted
down through my office basket, the janitor's barrel,
the trash packer's truck; then they'll gloat in the dump
where my best efforts find their freedom these days.

I will have changed another thousand times and still be
terrified of the glare of your approach. I will be still
standing here in layers, trying on selves as if I were
a fire sale—This roar must be me going up in flames.

So what should I be thankful for today? Poor bird, horse, man,
I've ruined everything. But I can't wait to see you once more.
Thank you. Thank you. Thank you.

It Hurts Everywhere

> *All the trouble of the world*
> *and my love over it*
> *like a naked beast.*
>
> — Paul Éluard

I'm here in this corner tonight, in black need, smoking,
sending up your wild name so it will find you.

If you do not come tonight, the tank with the mad driver
blazing at the slit will have me for another Poland.

I know you are out there: restless, testing the air,
lifting to sniff where the latest excitement is coming from.

I don't want this riot of hot rain and tension.
I want to sit down at a table again without saying table.

Right now, there must be someone in Idaho, wishing
for another life, whom I could fall in love with.

She makes me feel even worse.

Sitting upright in the 2 a.m. blackness, off-balance,
blank, I make the image of your body flower in the darkness.
Like the sun, I keep it alive by staring, at you tending
the colorful faces and wild plumage of what seems impossible
for me to grow. I've grown silent twisting with the houseplants
I keep dying of neglect.

Your garden rises in a slow commingling of sunlight
and laughter until I'm over my head, under the covers,
throbbing, thinking I can't stand this any longer.

I want to be buried in something totally unimportant
and not find your neck-twisting body at the bottom of it.
I want to find myself at the end of the day in love
with the simple curve of a comma, which I now see as a scythe.
I want a pause in which everything sighs and goes back
to normal: the miles of sunlight between us as simple
yellow space. The blackness, blank.

Today I Knew I Would Never Have You:

the lack of air, the high plane half-way
in another world, the unbearable heaviness
of climbing to my room which, like you,
won't stop drifting and yanking
at the top of its flight for freedom,
told me that.

A shred of cloud blew against the sun.
It was infinitely sad to no one,
except me, who happened to look up
and notice the day go out.
I thought of a bald man pulling
the chain on a bare light bulb
before bed, who rubs his eyes
in the mirror to make sure he's there,
then makes himself disappear.

All the time I was with you
untiringly waving my arms
just to get you to notice,
you took yourself aside and spoke
as a mother to her daughter
about what is right.
What is right?
Whatever I was feeling you rolled
in your mind's white palm
and smiled simply. It astonished me
that trying hard wasn't enough.

Just to drive off
with the bewildered survivor
in the rear-view mirror
who wouldn't let go
must have been hard.
Hard not to see him
getting smaller,
flickering in the sun
as he felt the unimaginable
future without you
take a deep breath.

Answers

Today the roses in the silver vase have opened their widest:
red and white faces blown back in a still room.

Even cut, they have the strength to surrender.
Their petals lie scattered like the silks of a courtesan.

I sit here tearing one after another, my thoughts
caught off-guard by my hands.

Living Inside a Dot

What good did it do dragging a bag across the whole U.S.
as if grabbing myself by the throat, just to end up living
inside the dot I thought you'd shrink to?

All day I sweep the city of my childhood, gulls, and ships
through the center of your eye and you don't see me.
When you were nothing to me, you looked and looked.

With you I found the one place in the world
where I could drop my heart down a hole, "Hello!"
and still hear it never hitting bottom.

You sleep, I wake up in the middle of the night. You cough
and they have to bring me water. I have a good mind
to forget you, but I'm afraid that I would disappear.

3. Wandering Among Women

> *I refuse—out of an incapacity that I elevate*
> *to a principle—to resist what I find irresistible.*
>
> — Philip Roth

The Instinct

A man feels humiliated
when his wife turns her private
landscape over and leaves him
falling through black space.

There is a horse kicking
in the mind that must be let out.
Men see it in each other's eyes
and hold onto their women.

Young girls who have ridden
this horse in their dreams
cross their legs, still burning,
and concentrate on small talk.

Once in a while, a stray woman
who can get over anything
opens her blouse and teases
the horse into following her home.
As she unlocks the door it occurs to her
how huge it will seem in the house.

Sometimes a man will punish his wife
with abstinence. The horse shrinks
into a small dog who rolls over
the edge of sleep while his master
wanders the house eating leftovers
and shouting to himself.

The woman who hears that
decorates her house and makes breakfast
like a wife in the old days.
She averts her eyes and serves him
a future that is possible
now that he has let her out.

I Am My Favorite Number

This year I am my favorite number.
33.
It's "The Year of the Professional Bowler,"
"The Year of Love."

I said if all my dreams come true,
I'll quit. I'll just be happy.

But I can't let the black ball go
or stand the bed up in the wall.
I'm professional,

sliding out form so smooth my body pours
around refusals and absorbs them.
I've been on the tour that long.

Next week at 34 my year is up.
I will have rolled the length of my luck
toward those spindly waists
and dropped through impossible odds.

I will have thrown myself with style
on the hardwood floor
and emptied the world of desire.

He scrubbed the carpet until each nub stood out
like the nipples of a virgin. He polished
the French glasses until they squealed
with the pleasure of holding back.
The ferns rose nobly in a chorus of ahhs
and soon the room, elevated in a ringing sound,
was ready.

He squinted into the silence of his expectations
when his ears perked up. He thought the telephone
was about to become hysterical. Suddenly
the room seemed too demanding. Too correct.
He began living in it as fast as he could.

By the time she arrived, prettied by lateness,
the silence rising from his bed roared
like an iron lung. He stood behind the door
shouting, "Shut up! Shut up!" She questioned
his name ever so softly. O how he hated her.

How to Love Your Body

There was always something obvious
I never understood about my body.
Which way? was its basic question.
The last minute! screamed my hair.
Don't bother with your face, my face
said when it had made up its mind
to remain confused.

But now I share it with a woman
who has taught it how to glide
inside while smiling with the mind
of a white porcelain bowl.

Now it runs toward middle age defiantly
darker and stronger than my brother's
whose body I worshipped and wished
broken, which turned me toward a life
of anxiety in art.

How ashamed everyone is of his body!
Thank God for clothes, their clothes
seem to say. If happiness is the state
of feeling nothing, then I'd answer, "Yes,
I'm fine."

All I ever unknowingly wanted to do
was to get back to my body,
to write home: Ma, I've written
a happy poem, which would disgust her
if she knew why.

I suppose, like me, you'd give anything
to pull out the dark sticks of regret
on which you've hung your body.
I'd like to hold you for a few minutes
underwater until your need for breath
was the woman you loved and you were willing
to give her up to learn how.

Wandering among women, sometimes my body flashes
through the great freedom of black internal space
and becomes dazzlement inside them.

Once it was the ocean that allowed me such enormity.
Now it is the open legs of women that everything I am
flies through. I am not sorry for this and it's true

that this flood from which only the body speaks
takes me further away from unhappiness than ever.
And I don't want love. This morning I am across

the street somewhere in America where a woman
has left me a silver pillowy balloon undulating
in mid-air like a brilliant wish.

Everything I am and ever valued has wandered free.
I want to come floating over the top of a new rise
every night, and be taken home, freed.

Sleep

The bats blow away like bits of paper
in a slipstream: I have no thoughts.

The bullfrogs gnaw on green balloons:
old men . . . old men . . . old men . . .

Waterstriders iron out the lake
until the clouds are smooth white sheets.

Inside the pike coast downward in a dream
past grim bass towing darkness to the bottom.

The underwater log of memory dissolves
into silt that settles on the voice in sleep.

You are plunging with the boulder of your heart
toward sleep. Holding on and letting go

of fears that squiggle out like tadpoles
until passing down through water is your breath.

Your clothing tumbles to the surface like thoughts
of giving up. Moon does the deadman's float.

All night dreams drag your sleep until
they lift you out like a dead body and weep.

It's another night made up of you, thin as cells
spreading out across the lake in links.

Lake flashes her dark body inside-out. She grins.
You pour through yourself, spilling nothing.

A Dress in the Wind

The wind blows a woman's dress through the air.
Whose flag is this that seems so troubled by wishes?
Who has let go? Someone is doomed to eat the hollow
stare of the moon while the dress coils, unfurls, and rolls
through the air, teaching the emptiness of desire.

All the mounted head of deer seem lost in a dream.
The wind must have snagged in their antlers
as they lowered their heads and, plunging through red,
emerged to possess the stillness of winter trees.

Intricate rosettes of wishes swirl in the wind. The trees
rock and grunt awake, issuing fiery green flags that wave
in the natural anthem. Because someone has taken off her dress
and let go, the world is out of control.

The Fantasy

There's a woman on a hill with a light summer dress on
lying on her stomach, reading something very far away
from sex. The stars in their blackness can't penetrate
the day for she is under the blaze of the one human star
as a man lifts her dress and she goes on reading and thinking
the wind is like a man's hand and whatever is happening
above and behind her as the page turns over is a dream.

The man on the back of the blonde woman flying uphill
is looking at the spot where an explosion will take place
exactly when he gets there. As she closes her eyes, night
travels through the universe like the long weight of a man
coming down. For an instant the surprising taste of grass
flares in her like flashfires on a distant hill.

She dreams she is walking on the boulevard, wondering
if that man is her lover, or maybe that man. What is
the face of the wind? In a gorge in a country torn by war
a soldier absent-mindedly looks up at the stars, wondering
why perfection must be contained by such distance and silence.

She opens her eyes and sees white grass against a white hill.
There is a fluorescent silence such as attends the space
just after a scream. Blue struggles its way back into the sky.
The stars recede, growing fainter, like footsteps in a dream.

The Phenomenon of Combustion

I imagine the idea of a dress
was stolen from a flower
in the year fire was discovered.
But no one is positively sure.

So desire is a controlled explosion
in which need is faster than light
and more precise than fire.

If that sets a dress on fire
or flowers explode, who cares?
It's Spring and this is just
an idea for a love poem.

Although I've never seen her,
I make pieces of devotion
fill the darkness of her sleep.
She smiles to herself, I think.
It's an eclipse. But who hasn't been
blinded by someone lifting up her dress?

Such great danger and awe of beauty.
I'm unsure, the way children are
in the presence of a candle.
Intuitively they whisper, then—
well, I don't wish to blow it out.

All our lives, wet logs in a fire,
desire is under control.
I've allowed myself to ask for beauty
and like beauty it's unfair.
Good, we're even.

The phenomenon of combustion means
no one is positively sure.

Engram

The utterly beautiful remembers nothing
except the nameless crumbling of her clothes,
the look of their terrible damage.

Alone in a few of the thousands of nights
that will follow, you will feel her hand
still pressed against your back.
She was always alone.

Closing your eyes, you will experience
her absence, your absence, then absence itself.
Her name is a dark wood where you find yourself
calling out her name, then your own.
Without her now, you are everywhere.

A small part of you will never give this up.
A small part will go on.
None of this will ever occur to her.

Lightweight

The few times I've been knocked out cold
I wasn't interested in coming back. Not that
being a cold black speck in a miasma of stars
was so spectacular, I couldn't take the fullness
of the heart.

For the heart is a stubborn problem
whose silence is described by noise.
It's the roar of an empty stadium
with the face of a boxer's glove,
the two-fisted pout of a child
who pounds I will and I will not.

So I throw a cold shot down like a fist
smashed in my face. The booze hits my brain
like a bell. Everyone rises and drinks to the heart.
I call the bar my heart and drink to that woman
in the corner. Here's to the heart, to that soak
of darkness starred by list. Here's to all the hopeless
lovers in the world walking around knocked out.

4. Call To Be Left In The Air

All my life I've been coming home.

The Climb

for Marsh Terry

Facing the black drop of a mountainside,
everything screaming down,
sometimes it seems easier to cut the rope
the others climb and own the thrill of a fall,
then own nothing, forever, at all.

Except I see their faces are so much
like mine: my wife with her hand extended
has learned from the mountain what it is
to wait. I took this to mean weight.
My eldest son gets his life confused
with changeling clouds and can't hold on.
The tiny one sits in a niche and dreams
he's sitting in a niche. What could I be
without the stories of myself they tell?

When a friend's husband died,
she planned to go away. O anywhere!
But she regretted having to take
herself with her. Going or staying
became the same. So she went away.

For all I know this terrible climb
might be to the rest of the world
like standing in line to collect—
to those whose lives are truly terrible.
I only see the rock, the indiscernible
movement down below. Once in a while,
a shout circles from the other side
from one who has been at it so long
he's learned both to climb and look out.
I recognize that shout. It hits me
like my name. Then I feel the tugging
at the line as reassuring, and resume the climb.

Light Sips On Nothingness

It's always been like this:
a man leaves his family for one night out
though the weight he feels on his back
as he closes the door on his wife's embrace
is the hill the house once stood on.
So the house teeters on the edge
and years later as he drives by the darkened,
rocking house with its squat look of revenge,
he throws thoughts of the children out at them.

What is her pride if not the taking of revenge?
So she moves slowly through the things she left
unsaid and makes sure she'll never say them.
And if the evenings seem longer eating alone
she makes them longer by thinking everything
is over, that the empty bed in the mirror
is not the picture of a bed, but the reflection
of a blessing. There'll be no more second thoughts
of her standing in the mirror dressed to kill.

The questions children ask go clean through the heart,
arc around the world and go clean through again.
They want to know. Tell us why you're apart.
They stand there with your eyes as full authority.
The secret they hold is a shout. Love in the darkest
moment of a child's heart is simply light sleeping
with the lights on. They take aim by opening the heart.

Being Alive

You wake one morning, and the summer is dead,
but your eyes are still dazed by the tumultuous light
of yesterday, and in your ears you hear the roar of the sun
turned to blood. The color of the world has changed.

— Cesare Pavese

The small boy in the third row near the end
of the classroom wishes the future would arrive.
He feels keenly how it is to be someone, as he
heads over to the old man's variety store, certain
that someday he'll whistle down with both feet
inside a new man. The tune he whistles is a light
accompaniment to the history of the world.

The old man in the variety store is going blind.
He is waiting for some child to reach up to him
while the clouds that pass across his face bury him
in whiteness. Then he'll give out the wax lips and
mustaches so the little boy he's losing sight of
can run off wearing the expression of the immortals.

The small boy knows it takes an old man's strength
to hold down an empty street, that one slow shake
of an old man's head can erase a little boy. If only
the boy could change like the clouds, he could keep
the whiteness the old man sees before him. He tries
hard closing his eyes to make something of the darkness
inside him. He only feels how it is to be alive.

One day the old man stops in front of the school
to feel the sidelong glance of the afternoon light
weave in his glossy darkness the sweet smell of wax.
He listens with the stone posture of the turtle
to something so large it can't be heard. The old man,
light as a cloud, lets go of his love that tears off
like a land mass and passes through the air like air.
It makes the small boy look up to see who he'll become.

Natural Words

for my son, Seth

You, my little sea-chaser, you outrun words.
Remember the poets who gave up writing
to become their art, who performed before
the mirror of the world? Well, you jump to catch
the things your mind has lifted and everything
you catch shines louder than the light of words.

And when you're sad, ah, sombreros full of great,
thick tears wobble in your bed. Then you run
against yourself with mischief, and the dark
corners of the room rise up to meet you. You
count your crisscrossed feet; there are too many
feet in a world that won't stand still and you smile.

Whatever has leaked from my life, all my losses,
must have gone to create the deep blue peace
surrounding you. So when you wave goodbye
to the small outpost of your mother's smile,
come to the man whose huge hands and head
are suffused in the sunlight of your drawings.

I will stand you on my shoulders, beyond all
my expectations, and there in the yellow spell
of wordlessness, you will rise up and learn
all there is of holding on and letting go.

My Son Who Is Me

My son asks, "Father, are you a poet?"
He wants to write stories about men
falling apart when he grows up.
He has a body that thinks hard without words.

He wants to climb on top of the quiet lion
who guards All Possibilities and walk north
toward the choir of light he's heard
exists somewhere, if only he can go far enough.

House of lost buttons, crayons, and clay,
nothing is real. Your father sleepwalks
in his life beyond himself, accepting
everything that is not him as real.

There is a small bird in a cold tree outside.
Anytime I pull the curtain back he's there.
He is all the sky above the streets to me.
He's the opposite of desire to the lost.

When you finally get your wish, you look back
at simplicity: there is a child saying what
he means, a man wishing for something else.
There is a bird, a child, a man lasting it out.

My sons sleep in a house without a father.
I sleep without my sons.
When I ask myself what's that like
I lose my balance.
I sleep without my sons.

Magnified in their dreams of me
coming closer, coming home, I hear voices
roaring and I'm on the phone:
"Hello, this is your father,

they shaved the horns of a bull today
which could feel the shadow of a man passing by.
The bull was blunted, lost direction,
ended up stumbling through a sword."

"Is there any message, father?"
"Yes. There's an enormity of darkness
out here. Tunnels thin as wire.
I can't get through."

I'm charging toward what I have to do,
receiving skulls on fire, tiny stick figures
from Valhalla, saying, "To Dad!"
Perennial Halloween.

All my life I've been coming home.
But that's another story.
It has nothing to do with you,
sleeping in a house without a father,
me, sleeping without my sons.
Whatever it is, it's begun.

Advice to my Sons: Go On

You've just learned to read
and someday when you look up
from a game where possibilities are
tagged out one by one until
you're the only one left standing,
you'll want to find out who you are
and then you might read this.
Go on.

You're Russian, English, and French.
You can't go home. Like any mongrel,
you'll have to make things solid
with your body, as I did you.
Mark what's yours and keep it
and keep others out. Follow your nose.
All laws are an abstraction of this
crassness: Pick out a tree and take a piss.
Go on.

But it's more complex. My trees are
words. Scraggly, wooden, second-growth.
They're what I mean. Through their changes
they've taught me what my limits are,
and the law they've given me is that change
is natural, although instinctively we fear it.
That's natural too. It's part of keeping.
Anything you choose will be hard getting through.
Go on.

I always counted every step it takes
to get from here to there. I never lost track.
I don't know why I did it, but it was
important. Billions of steps counted on.

We all do crazy things like that. It doesn't matter
what the ritual is; it's a way of getting out
of the unknown. I never forced your souls
toward God. Invent your own religion.
Go on.

And lastly, love. Now I'll say be careful.
There's nothing more incomprehensible
than a man in love. I'd warn you toward it
as I'd warn you toward your inmost self.
Be full of care, careful, not clever. Love
is all you'll know of self-fulfillment.
I'd warn you toward yourselves.
Go on.

5. Living Alone

To you is left (unspeakably confused)
your life, gigantic, ripening, full of fears,
so that it, now hemmed in, now grasping all,
is changed in you by turns to stone and stars.

— Rilke

Another Coil

for that one who dropped dead in his tracks when he asked
and nobody answered

— Vincente Aleixandre

I have lived up here for two months and know no one.
That window across the way from mine is my sun.
I think someone over there must also look out at himself.

Today I can hear his dull yellow wall hand up the message
"No," as if bending back like this I were a question.
When I was a boy I thought I could walk through walls.

Sometimes it pleases me to stand on the balcony undressed
and listen to the hum of the voltage towers in the fog.
I get quietly thrilled under the mild, cold moon.

Then I go inside and hear a door slam. Someone's home.
From somewhere the heavy cooking of soups and meats
opens up my childhood and waking I feel glad.

After days my woman knocks and for an instant I can't see her.
There is so much noise and light I hold her as if something
terrible had happened in the middle of a very nice day.

She tells me that I'm sighing again. I'm sorry. I must allow myself
these long oars pulls across the room. It's not because of her.
It's almost not me. The old man weaving blue rope inside me
has told me that he's finished with another coil.

Living Alone

At first you are starred by courage,
sparkling as the inside of a bulb.
Your fingers narrow into thin shafts
of laughter, a perfect fit.

Someone who passes for your double
cooks and cleans and chats endlessly
about your life. Then one night an outsider
shows up; but next morning she stretches
and returns through the enormous world.

In nine months a high pitched sound
sleeps in the room with you. The stars
are dreaming with the eyes of mice.
So you break down a little and drink alone.
It's a celebration to launch you
back inside yourself, that stone wall
on the other side of the world.

What was so important about living alone
you ask. Everything is backward in the mirror
you avoid. It would be a miracle to have
someone to touch. So you imagine being
on the move, glittering darkly, all edges,
like a hunter. You have a desperate gift
to give someone, but you want to live alone.

Mockingbird, Copy This

Mockingbird, I've been working hard
on a small routine,
a series of one-liners,
a word meant to keep me going,
please keep me going,
toward what I am.

I heard your woman sort of moan
behind your song.
But it's a job, isn't it,
the same old song
that God performed
when he made himself appear:
I Am Who Am.

Some God. Delusions of grandeur,
dissatisfactions, loneliness
that keeps us changing
a rivulet of whistles
into a river, a world,
the same old song.

Mockingbird, I don't know how you sleep.
I imagine you just hang on,
eyes wide open,
until the first star appears
then you sleep in its billion
blinking echoes.

I won't ask if you're happy.
Don't ask me.
But there's such a thing
as courage.
It's in your gaiety.
That's what I listen to.
Then sing.

What Comes Naturally?

I've never found anything easy.
Even doing nothing tears me up.
And just getting drunk disgusts me,
so I drink again to forget.

But I love the way the cool moon twirls
in the exotic blackness of space—
O tiny happiness of stars, I want a woman
to make love to, even an imaginary woman,
from whom my mind doesn't veer away.

I feel like a vestigial piece of the heart
that's broken off and goes wandering the streets
without pleasure. In this town the women and cops
all laugh, which is why I don't breathe when I'm near them.
That's another way I've discovered to stop thought.

I don't know what's wrong with me,
why things aren't easy. I wake up thinking
this could be a great day and the other half
of me thinks No, this *is* a great day.
But the rest of me knows it won't be easy.

Knock Turn

Everything's important and nothing matters.
That's how I learned to be a man, years of
hanging in the streets, learning how to
stand and take it, give it, get it back.

Each night we'd go for something big and crazy
at the wide end of experience, so we'd have something
famous to talk about, make the sun shine off our teeth.

I woke up damaged from that sleep
and found that people don't even have the kindness
to say, I know what you mean. I'm no fool.
You know what I mean.

Tonight the summery sounds of punches and shouts
rise again from the darkened golfcourse, and again
I'm kicking at the chest of what is now
the town undertaker. My God, the undertaker,
whose name was Bill. He knew he'd have another chance
to lay me out.

So I sat in a little black tree loaded
with ripe cherries and just closed my eyes.
All I heard was bells. That's how I learned
a hundred kinds of silence can take the place
of things not done.

It was important pretending nothing mattered,
killing time at the height of a scream.
Everyone wins and nothing is won.
Now I treat myself like a son.

Something Else

In this small room I'm beginning to feel
as if they're hunting me down.
The mirror has doubled the size
of the opposite wall which goes on
forever saying nothing that refreshes me.

But what pleasures did I memorize today?
The glance that beautiful woman gave me
was a gift. There are so many beautiful faces.
I think each one must be thinking
some wonderful thing.

Yesterday I saw a wild composer play Ravel
with two different shoes on,
stepping on stars, stepping on wind.
I attribute his passionate performance
to absent-mindedness, which I've got.

Just because I don't care what I look like
today in this city of beautiful faces,
anything seems possible. I could fly,
tunnel, walk, or remain seated.
I can go out or stay in.

Only sometimes I get so hungry for a woman
I sit in a public place. I must look
desperate because the dogs stop sniffing
and veer away. I wonder what desperation
smells like until I enter my room.

Once I lived without desire. Now I wake
with fistfuls of silk and am astonished
it's just a trick of light. My desire
is no bigger than a pinpoint of light
in the eyes, yet it floods the world.

Now more than ever my life seems just
a sublimation of something else.
I could follow the dark splashes of desire
all the way down to their names
and still never get there, never give up.

Tonight I'll wander like a lovestruck boy
leashed by desire. The stars have come out
like beautiful prospects, faces in a doorway.
The coiled power of living alone is in me
and anything can happen. Anything will.

On Nights Like This

On nights like this I'm happy
simply being still.
It's a small happiness
like my mother's hand
brushing back my hair.
Even a child's peace of mind
can seem enormous.

When I was a boy I loved to stare
into the velvet-lined cases
of accordians and guitars.
Something that contains music
feels deeper than music,
darker than all the instruments
I threw away.

That left me by myself
wishing the wind would tear
layer after layer of me
in someone's direction. And I admit once
I tried to throw myself away.

But tonight I'm finding it
in my heart to forgive myself.
God knows why.
I lift the darkness, step inside,
and imagine the sun
hour after hour
slowly brush across the sky
until it's empty.

It's such a small happiness,
so much has passed,
I hold both hands.

Pull for the Horizon, It's Better Than Nothing

a line from the song, "Shipwreck"

This is what I taught myself:
that the line of emptiness
where the sky falls welded
to the empty sea isn't nothing.
Pull out of your sleep.

Look at your hand. Really look.
Something has dragged itself across,
crossed it loaded down,
and recrossed at high velocity,
as if even before you were born
something was searching for you.

Now close your hand and forget.
You have the face of the wanderer.
The fist. The slamming of doors
marches all the way down to the horizon
which recedes as you approach,
stops when you sleep,
grows up your back.

Telepathic Note to Poet Friends

Friends, I'm lonely today.
Nothing's broken, only today I have no bones
and this softness needs an escort toward its death.
So I'm watching the slow tarantellas of the snowflakes
wink and go out, thinking you've been crushed by less.

Lately I've admired the classic themes
of western movies: silence, practice, and space.
Each of us has waited for *it* to happen,
no matter what. It doesn't matter what.
It all comes down to facing a gun
and trying to say it while the sun fires away,
the horses melt, and next door a woman shrieks
a perfect poem at her kids. In other words,

we've all spent years in rooms snowing darkness,
packing it into the shapes of music, or maybe lovers.
So somewhere far off I hear a black piano resound
in sympathy. All I wanted to say, my friends, is
I'm amazed that you're still singing.

Winging It

They try having each other without pain,
try sparing each other the embarrassment
of lifting an empty glass to drink,
of reaching for a hand that's moved,
of having to part by the clock, unhealed
and throbbing against their clothes.

— Barbara Orlovsky

You and the woman under you
shove off behind closed eyes
and say in unison, "Take me there."

It looks awkward—
two different wings
fused against a great idea.

But the opening of this gift
is half the gift.
The rest is light, a flash

that slows the most delicate gesture
to a roar which pulses out
like ripples in a pond
and moves the stars a little.

* * * *

Ever since I was born
there's been an angel tumbling to earth.
One wing has landed in a tree
though it looks like a bird
has torn itself free
and taken off.

Either I'm invincible
or something in me has given up.

Under the crackle and blare,
my woman whispers, "What's the message?"
And I find myself for no reason
saying, "Don't bother. Don't ask."

What is the question?

We are fire tearing from fire
and, reassured, we veer away.

* * * *

All those years I took
the whitened cryings of the mind
for silence.

Then what did I hear?

I want to blow out the sun and drift awhile,
for sometimes darkness is a mirror
you can walk into and, turning around,
light up the world.

From here middle age is a wilderness
which looks exactly like the world.

The Author

Jack Myers was born in Lynn, Massachusetts, in 1941. He received his M.F.A. from the Iowa Writers Workshop. In 1977 *The Family War* won The Texas Institute of Letters Voertman Award and was recognized by The Great Lakes Association as one of the finest small press books published that year. His work has appeared in over one hundred magazines and journals and has been frequently anthologized. Currently, he is Associate Professor at Southern Methodist University in Dallas and a field faculty member at Goddard College in Vermont.